THE LIBRARY OF
AMERICAN
LIVES AND TIMES™

JOHN ADAMS

Patriot, Diplomat, and Statesman

Miriam Gross

The Rosen Publishing Group's
PowerPlus Books™
New York

For Martin

Published in 2005 by The Rosen Publishing Group, Inc.
29 East 21st Street, New York, NY 10010

First Edition

Editor's Note: All quotations have been reproduced as they appeared in the letters and diaries from which they were borrowed. No correction was made to the inconsistent spelling that was common in that time period.

Library of Congress Cataloging-in-Publication Data

Gross, Miriam.
John Adams : patriot, diplomat, and statesman / Miriam Gross.— 1st ed.
   v. cm. — (The library of American lives and times)
Includes bibliographical references (p.) and index.
Contents: Personal history — Early legal career — Starting a family — Stirrings of a revolution — Retaliation and war — Independence — To France — Europe again — Victory and peace — Back home to America — Party politics — The presidency — A long retirement — Timeline.
ISBN 1-4042-2649-4 (lib. bdg.)
1. Adams, John, 1735–1826—Juvenile literature. 2. Presidents— United States—Biography—Juvenile literature. [1. Adams, John, 1735–1826. 2. Presidents.] I. Title. II. Series.
E322 .G767 2005
973.4'4'092—dc22

                            2003017929

Manufactured in the United States of America

CONTENTS

1. Personal History .5

2. Early Career and Family Life 12

3. Stirrings of a Revolution 18

4. Retaliation, War, and Independence 32

5. An American Diplomat Abroad 45

6. Victory and Peace 63

7. Back Home to America 76

8. The Presidency .84

9. A Long Retirement 94

Timeline 100
Glossary 103
Additional Resources 105
Bibliography 106
Index 107
About the Author 109
Primary Sources 110
Credits .112

1. Personal History

John Adams came of age at a time when the world was changing, and through his courage and his values he helped to shape his world. Although he was born into a modest farming family in Braintree, Massachusetts, through his ambition and passion for justice, Adams became one of the most important figures in the American Revolution, and the second president of the United States.

The first of John Adams's ancestors to arrive in America was his great-great-grandfather Henry, who came to Massachusetts in 1638. Henry Adams had been a farmer in Somerset, England. With his wife Edith and their eight children, he sailed across the Atlantic Ocean to settle on his own land. He had purchased a tract of 40 acres (16 ha) at Mount Wollaston, 6 miles (10 km) outside of Boston. In 1640, this town became part of Braintree.

Opposite: John Adams sometimes said that all he wanted was to be a farmer, but his ambition carried him much farther. In his life, Adams was a lawyer, a Revolutionary statesman, an ambassador, the United States' first vice president, and its second president. John Trumbull painted this oil-on-canvas portrait of John Adams around 1793.

Henry's son Joseph inherited the land. He made a respectable living farming and brewing beer, as his father had. He also served as a town selectman and as a surveyor of highways. The next two generations lived a similar life, as farmers and occasional brewers. Each generation did a little better than the one before it. John Adams's father, also named John, became a lieutenant in the local militia and a deacon in Braintree's Congregational Church. He eventually left the farm his great-grandfather Henry had bought and moved into a four-room cottage in the same town. In 1734, he married Susanna Boylston and had three sons with her. John was the oldest, born on October 30, 1735. His brother Peter was born in 1738 and Elihu in 1744.

The Adams boys spent much of their childhood out-doors, playing with other children in the forests and rolling hills of Massachusetts. They also loved to hunt. They learned to use firearms at an early age, as did most boys growing up in the country at that time. They quickly became skilled at shooting squirrels, rabbits, wood-chucks, quail, and wild turkeys.

John began his education in a one-room school in a local teacher's house, where the boys and girls of the town read and recited passages from a schoolbook known as the New England Primer. At the age of ten, John was sent to the Latin School, where boys bound for a higher education were sent to prepare for college.

The Adams family farm is located in Braintree, later Quincy, Massachusetts. The Adams family lived in this community for nearly three hundred years. G. N. Frankenstein painted this watercolor of the farm in 1849. John Adams was born in the house on the right. Adams's son John Quincy was born in the house on the left, which was where the elder Adams raised his family.

John's brothers were training to become farmers, but his parents hoped to send John to Harvard to become a minister.

John was a poor student who often daydreamed through his classes or sneaked away from school to hunt or fish. He hated the Latin School's teacher, Joseph Cleverley, whom he found boring and mean. John's younger brothers and most other boys in the town were training to become farmers, and he longed to spend his days outdoors as they did.

Although John hated school, his father was determined to send the boy to Harvard. One day, his father asked John what he wanted to be when he grew up. "A farmer," John told him.

To demonstrate what a hard life lay ahead for a farmer, John's father took him out to a swamp to cut reeds for thatch. They spent all day hard at work in the hot sun, knee-deep in mud, and bitten by flies and mosquitoes. When they returned that evening, the elder Adams asked his son, "Well, John, are you satisfied with being a farmer?"

"I like it very well, sir," John answered.

"Ay, but I don't like it so well," his father said, "so you shall go to school today."

Deacon John then found his son a new teacher, Joseph Marsh, and the boy quickly improved in the private boarding school that Marsh ran. John began to love reading and studying with a passion that grew throughout his life. At the age of fifteen, John traveled 12 miles (19 km) by horseback to the village of Cambridge, Massachusetts, to take the entrance exam for Harvard. He was afraid of disappointing his father and Mr. Marsh, but he did very well and was accepted. He began Harvard the following fall, in 1751.

Life at Harvard followed a very strict routine. The day began at 6:00 A.M. with breakfast and prayers. Classes and study lasted from 8:00 A.M. until 5:00 P.M., with a short break for lunch. More prayers followed the

Paul Revere engraved this view of Harvard's campus around 1767.
Josh Chadwick created this reproduction around 1900. From left to right
Harvard Hall, Stoughton Hall, Massachusetts Hall, Hollis Hall, and
Holden Chapel can be seen.

afternoon classes, then a light supper at 7:00 P.M., then studying late into the night.

Many students at Harvard became either lawyers or clergymen. John's father wanted him to be a minister. Although it was a difficult decision, John felt that practicing law would give him more freedom to read and to pursue his own interests. John had also begun to long for fame and honor, and he hoped to become a great man. "Shall I look out for a Cause to Speak to," he wrote in his diary, "and exert all the Soul and all the Body I own, to cut a flash, strike amazement, to catch the Vulgar?"

The oldest college in America, Harvard was founded in 1636 in Cambridge, Massachusetts, as a school for young men training to be Puritan ministers. The college was named for the Puritan minister John Harvard, who, upon his death in 1638, donated his library and one-half of his estate to the institution.

In its earliest years, the entire school consisted of nine students and one master. By the early eighteenth century, the college had grown much larger, and it expanded its course of studies to include natural science and moral philosophy. It began to attract many more students, though the rate of higher education in the American colonies was still very low. Only .5 percent of men, and no women, attended college in the colonies.

Harvard has since become one of the most distinguished universities in the world. It counts forty Nobel Prize winners and seven former U.S. presidents among its alumni.

Although John Adams longed for fame, his New England Puritan upbringing led him to feel guilty about his ambitions. Throughout his life, Adams struggled to control his vanity and pride.

After Adams graduated from Harvard, he took a job teaching school in Worcester, Massachusetts, to raise money to pay for his legal training. Worcester was about 50 miles (80 km) west of Boston and was a larger town than Adams had ever lived in, and he found it gloomy in the beginning. At first he saw teaching as a dead end, but he remembered his own unhappiness in the schoolhouse as a boy and tried to ignite a love of learning in his students. He began to enjoy observing the students, and he wondered which students would "turn out in his future Life, a Hero, and which a rake, which a phylosopher, and which a parasite."

After one year, Adams began studying law under James Putnam, Worcester's leading lawyer. For the next two years, Adams spent all of his time teaching, studying, and attending court sessions. In October 1758, at the age of twenty-three, Adams visited Boston to seek the advice of the city's most prestigious lawyers. He received a warm welcome and an introduction to the higher circles of law from Jeremiah Gridley and James Otis Jr., who would become his mentors.

2. Early Career and Family Life

John Adams began his law career in Braintree, Massachusetts, at the age of twenty-three. His first year of practice was hard, and he lost his first case. This failure left Adams depressed and discouraged. He worried that his peers and community would laugh at him and think he was ignorant. He was also angry with himself for not having prepared well enough for the case. To prevent such mistakes in the future, he rededicated himself to his studies.

Adams realized that in order to attract more clients, he needed to make a name for himself in his town. In 1761, two years into his legal career, Adams took up the popular cause of temperance. Although Adams drank moderately himself, he campaigned to close some of Braintree's taverns, which many people in town felt were a public nuisance. He also campaigned to prevent pettifoggers, or people practicing law without a license,

Next Page: This 1775 map of Massachusetts shows the areas in which young John Adams traveled, lived, or worked. These cities and towns (*circled*) include Braintree, Worcester, Boston, and Cambridge.

from representing clients. These causes helped Adams to obtain the recognition he longed for, and his caseload began to increase. He developed a reputation as a fine lawyer. In 1761, he was admitted to the superior court of his province.

Adams's life changed when his father died in May 1761. Deacon John Adams was the victim of an influenza epidemic that killed sixteen others in Braintree. Adams wrote the obituary, describing his father as "a man of strict piety, and great integrity; much esteemed and beloved wherever he was known, which was not far, his sphere of life being not extensive."

Although his father's death saddened Adams, it left him with one-third of his father's estate. He inherited a house and 40 acres (16 ha) of land. He loved the land and threw himself into projects for improving the farm. He enjoyed working in the fields, and he cherished the sense of independence and self-sufficiency that the farm gave him. Owning land made Adams a citizen and a taxpayer, which entitled him to speak and to vote in town meetings. He was also eligible for public office.

Adams had now reached the age at which many men would settle down, but his mentor Jeremiah Gridley had once warned him against marrying early. Gridley advised him to concentrate on the law instead and to build his reputation and career before starting a family. Adams took these words to heart when he fell in love with Hannah Quincy, who seemed to return his affections. The two visited with each other often, even speaking of marriage, but he warned her that he would have a long struggle establishing his career, and that he could not marry for four or five years. Although Hannah agreed to these terms, John never actually proposed to her, and she eventually married another man. The loss of Hannah left him depressed, but

Benjamin Blyth created this pastel portrait of John Adams around 1766. Blyth also made a pastel portrait of Abigail Adams at this time.

he also thought he was better off without the distraction of romance. He wrote in his diary, "Let love and vanity be extinguished and the great passions of ambition, patriotism, break out and burn."

It was a long time before Adams developed an interest in any other woman. In 1759, he had met Abigail Smith, Hannah Quincy's second cousin and the daughter of an affluent Congregational minister. Abigail had struck Adams as a girl who was witty, but shy and sickly

Abigail Adams was about twenty-two years old when Benjamin Blyth created this 1766 pastel portrait of her.

compared to her second cousin. He met Abigail again two years later, when his friend Richard Cranch was courting her sister Mary. Then Adams noticed Abigail's independent spirit and deep intelligence as well as her beautiful dark eyes and black hair. Abigail admired her stocky, ruddy-faced suitor's assertiveness as well as his sense of humor. They shared a love of literature and spent hours discussing Shakespeare and Molière. When John traveled on legal business, they began writing letters, a habit that continued throughout their lives.

In October 1764, after a three-year courtship, John Adams and Abigail Smith married. John was twenty-nine and Abigail was twenty. By this time, she had become his best friend and closest confidant. She was a spirited and an independent woman, and her husband encouraged her independence. He valued her advice above anyone else's, on everything from farming to friendship to politics. Adams's career would keep them apart for most of their marriage, but, through her letters, Abigail remained a trusted influence on everything John did. Nine months after they were married, on July 14, 1765, Abigail gave birth to their first child, a daughter they named Abigail and nicknamed Nabby. In July 1767, Abigail and John Adams had a son, John Quincy. Another son, Charles, was born in 1770, and another, Thomas Boylston, was born in 1772.

Adams's growing law practice frequently took him away from home, on cases about land transfers, murder, adultery, tarring and feathering, and insurance. As was typical for lawyers of his time, Adams traveled a legal circuit that extended as far as 200 miles (322 km), from the island of Martha's Vineyard, Massachusetts, to Maine in the North, and as far west as Worcester. He also spent a great deal of time in Boston.

3. Stirrings of a Revolution

Boston in the 1760s was a bustling city of about seventeen thousand people. The narrow, twisting streets held a lively intellectual culture that had established America's first public school in 1635 and its first newspaper in 1704. Boston also had a thriving shipping industry, which often brought Boston's political life up against the restrictive British trade measures. One of these measures was the writs of assistance, which Parliament tried to impose on American merchants. These were search warrants used to look for goods smuggled on board ships in violation of Britain's trade laws. Represented by James Otis Jr., a group of Boston's merchants sued to end the measure.

Much American anger against the British began in reaction to taxes. From 1754 to 1763, Britain fought France for control of American territory in what came to be known as the French and Indian War. This war, in addition to the Seven Years' War in Europe, left the British in debt, and they tried to raise money by taxing the American colonists. In 1764, Parliament passed the

Sugar Act, which put a duty on the colonial sugar trade and attempted to tighten shipping regulations. At this point much of New England's economy was based in shipping, particularly in the rum and molasses trades, and the new regulations posed an economic threat to the colonists. These taxes were usually evaded by American traders.

In 1765, Parliament passed the Stamp Act, which required a British stamp on every piece of paper, from legal documents and advertisements in newspapers to college diplomas and playing cards. The Stamp Act affected a larger segment of society than the Sugar Act

Benjamin Franklin created this woodcut for the May 9, 1754, *Pennsylvania Gazette*. It was part of Franklin's unsuccessful effort to unite the colonies against the French and Indian attacks on frontier settlements. This idea would resurface when the colonies stood together to fight for independence from the British in the American Revolution.

had, and it enraged many people. Even the hated royal lieutenant governor Thomas Hutchinson wrote to Parliament to protest the act. He asserted that the government had already given the colonies the right to make their own laws and to tax themselves.

On May 29, 1765, Patrick Henry gave an impassioned speech against the Stamp Act to Virginia's governing body, the House of Burgesses. This speech led to the passage of the Virginia Resolutions, which denied the right of the British government to tax the colonies. There were still a large number of loyalists, or Tories, in the American colonies who found the Virginia Resolutions to be extreme to the point of treason. Other colonists simply felt that taxes should be set only by representatives whom they elected themselves. Opposition to the British government, though controversial, was growing with the fear that other liberties would be lost along with taxation rights.

In Boston, Adams's second cousin Samuel Adams united two street gangs to protest the Stamp Act. They called themselves the Sons of Liberty and began a series of public demonstrations. With an effigy of stamp distributor Andrew Oliver, they paraded through the streets shouting "Liberty, Property, and no Stamps!" They made their way to Oliver's town house, which they broke into and vandalized. Oliver resigned from his position in fear of the mob, and twelve days later the Sons of Liberty targeted Hutchinson's mansion.

Although many people were shocked by the violence of these acts, a growing number of people were rallying under Otis's declaration that "taxation without representation is tyranny."

John Adams disapproved of the violent mobs, but he sympathized with the impulses behind the actions. On August 12, 1765, he anonymously published an essay in the *Boston Gazette* entitled "A Dissertation on Canon and Feudal Law." In this essay, he declared that freedom for the colonists was a right given by British law, as well as a natural right given by God. The essay was highly regarded and even was reprinted in England.

In October 1765, representatives from nine colonial assemblies met in New York City and formed the Stamp Act Congress. Under pressure from the Stamp Act Congress, the British parliament repealed the Stamp Act in the spring of 1766. After Jeremiah Gridley died in 1767 and James Otis Jr.'s health began to fail, Adams became the most prominent attorney in Boston. By 1768, he grew tired of the 6-mile (10-km) ride from Braintree to Boston, so he moved his family from Braintree and set up his own office in Boston.

Around this time, Adams received a chance for remarkable advancement. Jonathan Sewall, a friend from Harvard, had just become attorney general of the

Following Spread: William Pierie created *Views of the Area Around Boston, New England* in 1773. The map in the center is of the Boston area. The pictures surrounding the map depict several views of eighteenth-century Boston.

W FROM *DORCHESTER NECK*, at Station A.

W FROM *CHARLESTOWN*, at Station B

Roxbury

VIEW of *CASTLE WILLIAM* at Station

VIEW of *CASTLE WILLIAM* at Station D.

province, the highest legal office in the region, and he offered Adams the position of advocate general in the Court of Admiralty. Adams and Sewell came from similar backgrounds and had once had much in common. When the two young men were beginning their law careers in the 1750s, they wrote each other long letters about the struggles they faced. Now, however, they found themselves on opposite sides of a growing movement. Although Adams and his mentors Gridley and Otis were both opponents of Hutchinson, Sewall was a Tory and a leader in the royal governor's administration. Although it could have meant immediate success in his career, Adams could not accept a position in a system in which he did not believe. The two friends began to drift apart.

Although he sympathized with the Revolutionary cause, Adams was torn about his own involvement in politics. He worried about the effect his actions could have on his career and reputation. As a lawyer, part of him still felt loyal to the laws that the Sons of Liberty were protesting. He also worried about the motives behind Otis's and Samuel Adams's leadership. He felt tremendous admiration for both of the radicals, but, just as he always worried about his own sense of ambition, he also distrusted others who sought political power.

Despite his initial misgivings, Adams was swept into Boston's struggle against the British authorities in 1768, when he was chosen to defend John Hancock against smuggling charges. In 1767, the British government imposed the Townshend Acts, which put levies on all imports of British glass, lead, paint, paper, and tea. The British also created a board of customs, which inspected and recorded all imports. The Americans peacefully protested this measure at first by holding demonstrations in Boston and boycotting, or refusing to buy, British goods. Then John Hancock's ship the *Liberty* was seized for violating customs rules, and Hancock was charged with smuggling. Adams was chosen to be part of the defense team, and the case dragged through much of that winter. By the time the charges against Hancock were dropped, Adams wrote that he was "weary and disgusted with the Court, the Officers of the Crown, the Cause, and even with the tyrannical Bell that dongled me out of my House every Morning."

Finley Breese Morse painted this oil-on-canvas portrait of John Hancock (1737–1793) around 1816. Hancock was the first person to sign the Declaration of Independence. Hancock later became the governor of Massachusetts, serving nine terms.

The atmosphere in Boston was getting tense. Two British

regiments had arrived in October 1768. The townspeople resented their presence. Crowds in the street began harassing the British soldiers, and many brawls broke out as a result. Loyalists and customs informers were attacked, and their property was vandalized. The increasing violence and mob mentality worried John Adams.

On the night of March 5, 1770, these tensions turned deadly in an incident that is known as the Boston Massacre. It was a cold, moonlit night, with knee-high drifts of snow on the ground. Around nine o'clock, a small group of men and boys began taunting the single British soldier who was guarding the Customs House. A crowd started gathering around them and grew to several hundred people, some of them bearing sticks and clubs. When the guard was joined by eight other soldiers with loaded muskets and bayonets, the crowd threw snowballs, chunks of ice, oyster shells, and stones at them. As the mob became more violent, the soldiers fired into the crowd. Five men were killed.

Samuel Adams immediately seized upon the incident as a symbol of British tyranny. He helped to distribute an engraving by Paul Revere that depicted the incident as a slaughter of innocent civilians. He turned the funeral of the victims into a massive political demonstration.

The day after the incident, John Adams was asked to defend the soldiers. He was told that no one else would take the case. Although he realized that his decision would probably attract public scorn and suspicion,

Paul Revere's hand-colored engraving depicts a dramatized view of the Boston Massacre. Behind the British troops on the right is the Royal Customs House, marked with a sign reading "Butcher's Hall." Below the print are eighteen lines of verse that detail the incident and list the dead, or "unhappy Sufferers," and the wounded.

Adams believed strongly that every person in a free country should have the right to counsel and a fair trial. He took the case without hesitation.

After studying the events of that night, Adams believed that the soldiers were innocent of murder and had only acted in self-defense. In his closing statement at the trial, he blamed the five deaths on a violent mob, saying, "And why should we scruple to call such a people a mob, I can't conceive, unless the name is too respectable for them. The sun is not about to stand still or go out, nor the rivers to dry up because there was a mob in Boston on the 5th of March that attacked a party of soldiers."

Adams also blamed the royal government for the conditions under which the mob erupted, warning his audience that "Soldiers quartered in a populous town will always occasion two mobs where they prevent one. They are wretched conservators of the peace." He held Governor Hutchinson responsible for creating the violent atmosphere in the first place by stationing British soldiers in Boston.

After two hours of deliberations, the jury acquitted all but two of the soldiers. Those two were found guilty of manslaughter in self-defense. This charge was less serious than murder. They were branded on their thumbs as punishment.

The verdict outraged the public, and Adams was criticized in the *Boston Gazette*. He estimated that he

John Adams often worked from the study in his house. Adams took on all different types of cases, including land transfers, monetary disputes, and criminal cases. Adams, as Sewall described him, was as "honest [a] lawyer as ever broke bread."

lost almost half of his legal business as a result of his unpopular role in the trial. It also brought him more respect, however, as it demonstrated his unbiased integrity. The following summer, the Sons of Liberty helped to elect Adams as one of Boston's representatives to the Massachusetts legislature.

The next major event in the movement against British rule was again connected to taxes and imports. Colonial Americans were avid tea drinkers, as were the British. Because of the high taxes on British imports, most of the tea the colonists drank was smuggled to the colonies from the Netherlands. In 1773, the British East India Company found itself stuck with a surplus of seventeen million pounds (7.7 million kg) of tea. The company was in financial trouble. To save the company, Parliament exempted it from export regulations. The company sent 1,700 chests of tea to American ports.

Even with the remaining taxes, this tea was cheaper than the smuggled Dutch tea the Americans had been drinking. Colonial merchants resented the British East India Company's monopoly on legal tea imports and worried that the cheaper prices would ruin their smuggling businesses. The Sons of Liberty had already been trying to stop the importation of duted tea from England because they objected to the taxes. They also felt that if Britain could enforce this measure, there would be no end to the authority Britain could hold over the colonies. They sent threats to the Boston merchants who planned to accept the shipment from the East India Company. The ships carrying the tea had arrived in Boston, and they sat in the harbor under British protection.

The Sons of Liberty assembled a town meeting in Boston's Old South Meeting House. They demanded that the tea be returned to England, but Governor Hutchinson would not let the ships leave the harbor without being cleared by customs. If the tea was unloaded for customs clearance, it was as good as imported, and the colonists would have to pay duties on it. To prevent this importation, armed radicals stood guard at the harbor to make sure that the tea was not taken onto land. On the night of December 16, 1773, after three weeks of protest, the radicals took action. A small group of people dressed up as American Indians marched down to the waterfront. The group invaded the ships and spent the next three hours dumping tea overboard into the harbor.

Learning of the Boston Tea Party the next morning, Adams sensed its importance. "This is the most magnificent Movement of all," he wrote in his diary. "There is a Dignity, a Majesty, a Sublimity, in this last Effort of the Patriots, that I greatly admire. The People should never rise, without doing something to be remembered—something notable And striking. . . . I cant but consider it as an Epocha in History." To Adams, this symbolic act had moved the Revolutionary cause beyond the violence of mobs toward something more respectable. The defiance that led to the Boston Tea Party, combined with the brutality of its consequences, would draw Adams deeper into the politics of the American Revolution.

4. Retaliation, War, and Independence

In response to the Boston Tea Party, Parliament struck back with a succession of punitive laws known as the Coercive Acts, which the colonists called the Intolerable Acts. First came the Port Act, passed on March 31, 1774, which closed Boston's port to all ships except those carrying fuel and provisions. This measure put thousands of colonists out of work. Next came the Massachusetts Government Act, which put the British king in charge of selecting the colony's government council and superior court judges. The British monarchy now held power over every part of Massachusetts's government. The third measure was the Administration of Justice Act, by which British officers accused of crimes in the colonies were tried in Britain. The fourth act was a revival of the Quartering Act, which allowed British troops to occupy colonists' homes. The crown reinforced its authority in Boston with seven infantry and artillery regiments.

These harsh measures united the colonies against Britain. On June 17, the Massachusetts Assembly called for the colonies to gather to address American

Commissioner of Customs John Malcolm is shown being tarred and feathered in this 1784 print by François Godefroy. The colonists were angered by his enforcement of the Intolerable Acts. Tarring and feathering a person was often used as a public demonstration against a crime or an unpopular action. Although it did not usually cause serious injury to its target, it was effective as a form of public humiliation.

grievances. This Continental Congress was to be held on September 6 in Philadelphia, Pennsylvania. The Massachusetts Assembly chose John Adams and Samuel Adams as two of the five Massachusetts delegates to the Congress. John Adams worried that he lacked the political experience required for this duty, and he grumbled about the effect it would have on his business, but he was proud to be chosen.

Shortly before leaving for Congress, Adams ran into his old friend Jonathan Sewall. They took a walk together, and Sewall brought up the subject of the Continental Congress. He warned Adams that Britain was determined to have its way and that if the Continental Congress continued its course, it was headed toward a war that would destroy the colonies. Once again, Sewall tried to persuade Adams to join the loyalists. Once again, Adams refused. "The die is now cast," he told his old friend. "Swim or sink, live or die, survive or perish, [I am] with my country." This was the last time they would see each other for thirteen years.

The delegates to Congress, for the most part, still considered themselves loyal subjects of King George III. The idea of independence from Britain was not yet an issue, and the primary aim of the Congress was to win back the rights to which they were entitled under the British constitution. To this effect they passed the Declaration of Rights and Grievances. Congress adopted the Articles of Association, which declared an American ban on all British imports and threatened to halt American exports to Britain if Parliament did not repeal its oppressive acts.

After almost two months, Congress adjourned and Adams returned home to Braintree, where he had moved his family to escape the tensions in Boston. Militia units and minutemen, so called because they were ready for service in one minute's notice, were training in every village. Adams spent much of his time writing letters to the *Boston Gazette* under the name

Novanglus, Latin for "New Englander," on the constitutional grounds for colonial resistance.

On April 19, 1775, British troops marching to confiscate ammunition exchanged fire with militiamen in Lexington and Concord, Massachusetts. On their way back, the troops were attacked from behind stone walls by American farmers and militiamen. The incident left nearly one hundred colonists and seventy-three British soldiers dead. Two hundred more British were wounded or missing. If Adams had once wavered in his commitment to the American Revolution, the violence of this act ended any loyalty he still felt to the British crown. A few weeks later, Adams rode to Philadelphia, Pennsylvania, to take part in the Second Continental Congress.

Congress opened on May 10, 1775, in the Philadelphia State House. New delegates included John Hancock from Massachusetts, Thomas Jefferson from Virginia, and the famous Benjamin Franklin, who had just returned from London. America was now at war. One important aim of this Congress was to create a national army and to select its leader. George Washington struck Adams as the obvious choice. Observing him in the first Continental Congress, Adams admired the Virginian delegate's leadership abilities and believed that Washington was "noble and disinterested." As commander of Virginia's army during the French and Indian War, Washington had gained valuable military experience. Furthermore, the

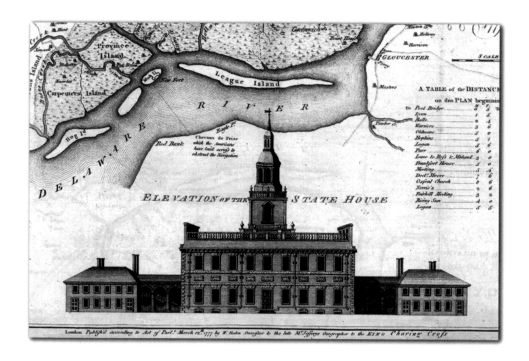

This engraving, entitled *A plan of the city and environs of Philadelphia*, was published by W. Faden in 1777. It shows how the State House looked in the late eighteenth century. The map in the background shows the Philadelphia area and the Delaware River, and includes the elevation of the State House.

fact that he was from Virginia would be important in gaining support for the war from the middle and southern colonies by easing fears that the Revolution would be dominated by the North. On June 14, 1775, Adams proposed Washington as commander in chief of the new Continental army. Samuel Adams seconded the motion, and the Continental Congress unanimously elected Washington.

Adams rose quickly to a leading role in Congress. His intelligence impressed the other delegates, and they often turned to him for guidance on the decisions they faced. He was a persistent and passionate speaker. He was also one of the hardest-working delegates, sitting on ninety committees and chairing twenty-five of them during the next two years.

As the war continued, the congressmen found themselves divided about its aim. Some delegates, such as John Dickinson of Pennsylvania, pushed for reconciliation with Britain and a return to the terms that had governed the colonies before 1763. Another group pressed for independence from Britain. When the Massachusetts delegation had first proposed independence at the opening of the second Congress in 1775, most of the other delegates considered the step too radical. As the war progressed during the next year, however, many more became convinced that independence from Britain was the only solution. Adams emerged as the leader of this group.

On July 1, 1776, Congress put the issue of independence to a vote.

This oil-on-canvas portrait of George Washington (1732–1799) by James Peale was painted around 1787, after the original 1779 painting by Charles Willson Peale.

Until the 1770s, few colonists seriously considered the idea of independence from Britain. Thomas Paine's pamphlet **Common Sense,** *published on January 9, 1776, brought enormous public support to the issue of independence.*

Paine wrote that hereditary monarchy was by nature evil and absurd, and that the colonists should forget about reconciliation with Britain. Paine argued that the American Revolution was about much more than taxes. The very principle of liberty was at stake, and the Revolution would give birth to a new era of freedom, with America becoming an "asylum for mankind."

As the floor was opened to discuss the issue, the Pennsylvanian delegate John Dickinson stepped forward. He argued that America could not survive without the support of the British Empire. He worried that Britain would try to enlist the help of Spain and France in the war against the colonies, and in return, would offer them pieces of American territory. Instead of fighting for independence, they should fight for reconciliation on American terms. A war fought for this goal would be shorter and less brutal and would have a more certain outcome.

Adams took the floor next. He argued that the colonists should sever their ties to the corrupt and tyrannous British crown. He said Americans would be better off governed by Americans than by rulers across the sea. He believed that morale would be higher throughout a long war if the colonies were fighting for independence. He also stressed the importance of foreign assistance, and that such assistance could only be granted to an independent nation. Thomas Jefferson later recalled that Adams spoke "with a power . . . that moved us from our seats." Richard Stockton, a delegate from New Jersey, called Adams "the man to whom the country is most indebted for the great measure of independency."

The debate continued into the night, and the vote was delayed until the next day. John Dickinson and another Pennsylvanian delegate were both absent that day. They could not bring themselves to vote for independence, but felt that since the measure would be passed it was better that the decision be unanimous. New York declined to vote as well, but all the other colonies voted in favor of independence.

The Virginian delegate Thomas Jefferson was already at work drafting a declaration of independence. He had begun his work in June, finishing his draft on June 28. The fact that Jefferson was from Virginia was also an important factor. As did Washington's, Jefferson's status as a southerner helped to balance regional influence among the colonies. Congress set about revising Jefferson's draft after deciding to declare independence.

John Trumbull painted his famous 1817 depiction of the signing of the Declaration of Independence for the Rotunda in the U.S. Capitol. Thomas Jefferson *(center)* is shown presenting the declaration to John Hancock *(seated on right)*, president of the Continental Congress. John Adams is standing directly behind Jefferson.

On July 4, 1776, Congress approved the final draft of the Declaration of Independence. The following morning, a printer made copies of the declaration, and it was printed in the *Pennsylvania Evening Post* on July 6. On Monday July 8, the declaration was read aloud in the State House yard. A crowd gathered and bells rang through the city. People lit bonfires on street corners and candles in their windows. Celebrations broke out all over the country as news of the declaration spread. The legendary signing took place almost one month later.

John Adams had been in Philadelphia for more than one year. The extended separation from her husband was hard for Abigail Adams, but John kept her updated on the progress of the war and of Congress through his letters. Abigail in her turn wrote to him with news of the family, as well as of the living conditions in Massachusetts. She also offered her husband advice on politics, including this warning about the new government:

> *I desire that you would Remember the Laidies, and be more generous and favorable to them than your ancestors. Do not put such unlimited power into the hands of the Husbands. Remember all Men would be tyrants if they could. If particular care and attention is not paid to the Laidies we are determined to foment a Rebelion, and will not hold ourselves bound by any Laws in which we have no voice, or Representation.*

Adams missed his family and at one point asked the Massachusetts Assembly to find a new delegate to replace him. The assembly refused, believing that Adams was irreplaceable. By summer 1776, many of the delegates were getting sick and were leaving Philadelphia. The constant work and pressure had gotten to John Adams as well, and he applied for a leave of absence. The war was going badly, however,

Abigail and John corresponded during their absences from one another. John wrote Abigail about political developments and Abigail updated John on the family's lives. At times she also gave him advice, as in this letter, in which she asks that the Continental Congress "Remember the Laidies" while drafting the Declaration of Independence.

Abigail faced many difficulties in running the farm in John's absence. It was difficult to find good farmhands to work on the farm. There were shortages of many household goods. The Adamses did not have a lot of money. Growing inflation meant that prices rose faster than people's incomes did. Abigail also longed to be reunited with John. Despite these hardships, Abigail saw it as her patriotic duty to maintain a well-run household as much as it was John's patriotic duty to serve his country in Philadelphia.

and Adams decided to stay in Philadelphia and do what he could.

One of Adams's most important roles in Congress was in helping to direct the war effort as a member of the Continental Board of War and Ordinance. The British troops and the German mercenaries who fought alongside them were highly trained professional soldiers, supported further by Britain's powerful warships. America had no warships, and the Continental army suffered badly from a lack of supplies, including arms, ammunition, shoes, soap, and medicine. Their morale was worn down by the lack of pay, as well as by diseases, such as smallpox, that ravaged the camps.

Adams and the other four members of the war office were responsible for appointing and promoting officers, recruiting soldiers, and obtaining supplies.

Adams also took an active role in the debates over the Articles of Confederation, the framework of government that would officially unify the colonies. He believed that unity among the colonies was important in the fight to gain independence and vital in maintaining that independence once it was won. His friend and fellow delegate Benjamin Rush stated the case eloquently, telling Congress, "We have been too free with the word independence. We are dependent on each other—not totally independent states. . . . When I entered that door, I considered myself a citizen of America."

5. An American Diplomat Abroad

Adams returned from Philadelphia to his family in Braintree on November 11, 1777. He intended to refuse reelection to the Continental Congress and to stay home and care for his family. Two weeks later, however, Congress sent a letter appointing him commissioner to France. He was to replace another agent, Silas Deane, on a mission to gain military support from the French and to forge a French-American alliance. This was a frightening prospect for Adams, as he did not speak French, had never left America, and was untrained in diplomacy. Despite his fears of failure and reluctance to leave his family once again, he felt that he could not refuse his patriotic duty to serve his country.

Taking with him his ten-year-old son, John Quincy, Adams left for his trip on a stormy February morning. He had never been to sea before, and they were about to embark on a 3,000-mile (4,828-km) journey in the most violent season of the year. Adams and his son boarded the twenty-four-gun frigate the *Boston* on February 13, 1778, but the weather prevented them from setting off for another thirty-six hours. When they stopped in Marblehead on the Massachusetts coast to take on more crew members, they got stuck for another forty-eight hours waiting out a snowstorm that had struck eastern Massachusetts.

This portrait of John Quincy Adams (1767–1848) was created by John Ramage around 1789. Adams's eldest son was a source of pride. John Quincy went on to become a diplomat, secretary of state, and the sixth president of the United States.

The captain of the ship was a thirty-year-old New Englander named Samuel Tucker. Captain Tucker was told to consult John Adams on every matter. Although he knew nothing of life at sea, Adams had a great deal of advice for the captain, and Tucker took it well. Adams's chief concerns were the lack of discipline among the sailors and the terribly unsanitary conditions. He knew from his work with the Continental army how a lack of cleanliness led to the spread of diseases such as smallpox. He also complained about the crew's swearing.

The weather posed a threat to a ship at sea in the winter, but sailing during wartime was even more dangerous. British warships patrolled the waters, and meeting one could mean either death or captivity. On the second day at sea, the lookout spotted three British ships on the horizon. The British ships began chasing the *Boston*. Captain Tucker evaded two of the ships, but the third followed close behind them for two days. Just as the ship closed in on them, a violent storm struck, allowing the *Boston* to escape. The storm that saved them brought new dangers, however. A bolt of lightning hit the main mast and injured twenty men.

The *Boston* brought John Adams from Boston to Bordeaux in the winter of 1778. The passengers and the crew endured snowstorms, lightning, and a skirmish with the *Martha*. Rod Claudius created this modern-day painting of the Boston around 1963.

Once the storm cleared, the *Boston* began making good progress. Adams and John Quincy made friends with a French surgeon on board named Nicholas Noel. Adams passed much of his time observing the habits and lifestyle of the crewmen, and he dined every night with the captain. Eventually, life at sea developed a routine, and the routine grew boring. "We see nothing but Sky, Clouds, and Sea," Adams noted, "and then Sea, Clouds and sky."

Then one day the *Boston* gave chase to an armed British merchant ship called the *Martha*. Captain Tucker ordered the passengers below decks, but John Adams sneaked back up with a musket in his hands. The *Boston* fired once, and the *Martha* fired three times. The captain angrily asked his passenger why he had exposed himself to danger. Adams smiled and said, "I ought to do my share of the fighting."

The *Boston* finally reached France through the port of Bordeaux on Monday, March 30. After six weeks and four days at sea, John Adams and his shipmates arrived in France to discover that the French-American alliance had already been formed before they left Massachusetts. Adams's job was now to join the other commissioners, Benjamin Franklin and Arthur Lee, in Paris to work out the details of the alliance.

Adams was awestruck at the sight of the landscape around him. He wrote in his diary that night, "Europe, thou great theater of arts, sciences, commerce, war, am I

Benjamin Franklin enjoyed this view from the terrace of his apartment in the Hôtel de Valentinois in Passy. Franklin lived in the hotel during his time as an ambassador to France and even witnessed the Montgolfier brothers' famous first balloon flight in 1783, shown in this colored engraving.

at last permitted to visit thy territories." He stayed four days in Bordeaux and saw a play and his first opera. When he left for Paris, a huge crowd gathered around to see him off, saluting him with thirteen cannon blasts.

Observing his surroundings on the journey to Paris, Adams was impressed by the quality of the roads and the fact that every field was being used to grow crops, in contrast to the vast empty spaces in America. Paris was by far the biggest city he had ever been in, and he was impressed by its grand churches and public buildings, as well as its well-tended gardens and elegant mansions.

On his first morning in Paris, Adams went out to see Benjamin Franklin in Passy, a suburb on the road from Paris to the Royal Palace in Versailles. Franklin lived in the magnificent Hôtel de Valentinois, and he was attended by nine uniformed servants. Franklin was hugely popular in France, and his friends were among the most influential figures in Parisian society. Crowds cheered him in the streets, and the image of his face adorned medallions and the lids of snuffboxes. His customary bearskin hat was even adopted by fashionable Parisian women. Although he was most famous for his inventions and electrical experiments, he was also seen as a wise man from the American wilderness.

At Franklin's insistence, Adams moved into a room in the Hôtel de Valentinois and became acquainted with Franklin's influential friends. Adams was amazed by the great wealth in France, the jewels and luxuries on display, and by the careful attention to personal appearance. As a New Englander of modest, plain tastes, Adams did not entirely approve of these luxuries. He wrote to Abigail, "I cannot help suspecting that the more elegance, the less virtue in all times and countries." He was charmed by the French and by their friendliness, politeness, and enjoyment of life. He was also impressed with French education and the intelligence of French women, who were more outspoken than were most American women.

Shortly after arriving in France, Adams discovered some serious divisions within the American commission. Franklin and Lee had been working together in Paris since December 1776, and they did not get along. Lee hated the French and was suspicious of nearly everyone he met. Lee believed that Franklin was thoroughly corrupt, and Franklin believed that Lee was ill-tempered and difficult to work with. Adams had come to France with great respect and admiration for Franklin, but after several weeks in his presence, he was disappointed by the man's character. He found Franklin careless with money, lazy, and poor in his command of the French language. Franklin was also too afraid to offend the French ministers, and therefore he asked very little of them. Adams felt it was necessary to be direct about America's need for more help from France's navy.

Much of the ministers' business was done with the Comte de Vergennes, France's foreign minister. Adams found Vergennes evasive and arrogant. Vergennes was annoyed by Adams's persistence and outspokenness. Although these qualities helped Adams in the Continental Congress, where his fiery speeches inspired others to join the Revolutionary cause, his personality was not suited for diplomacy. In European courts, business was conducted with subtlety and patience. Adams's directness made him annoying to many of the people that he worked with. They found him ungracious and temperamental.

Gustav Lundberg painted this portrait of the Comte de Vergennes (1719–1787) around 1774.

Adams found his work in France frustrating. There was little word from Congress in Philadelphia, and it took at least six weeks for any messages to arrive, assuming the ships carrying the letters were not first captured at sea by the British. It could take up to six months to receive an answer to any questions about what the commission should do. Adams spent his time trying to organize the commission's accounts, writing letters to gain support for America, and keeping up with events of the war through newspapers from London. He was upset by the image the British presented of him. "The English have got at me," he wrote to Abigail on February 13, 1779. "They make fine Work of me—fanatic Bigot perfect Cypher not one Word of the Language aukward figure uncouth dress no Address, no Character cunning hard headed Attorney. But the falsest of it all is that I am disgusted with the Parisians."

Adams felt terribly lonely in Paris. He was farther from Abigail than he had ever been, and letters between them took a long time to arrive. Although Adams claimed that he had written Abigail almost fifty letters, only two letters reached her. She wrote to him, "All things look gloomy and melancholy around me. You could not have suffered more upon your voyage that I have felt cut off from all communication with you."

On February 12, 1779, word reached Paris that Congress was disbanding the American commission, leaving only Franklin there as minister plenipotentiary, the diplomat with the sole authority to negotiate a treaty. Adams had suggested this change to Congress, feeling that it was a waste of public money to have the three ministers there, and he had even suggested Franklin as the plenipotentiary. The dismissal depressed him, however, and he felt that Congress had shown no gratitude for all the work he had done. Arthur Lee was sent on a new assignment to Madrid, Spain, but Congress left no instructions for what Adams was supposed to do next. He began making arrangements for his passage home.

Adams and John Quincy finally set sail for America on June 17, 1779, and arrived in Braintree on August 2. Adams was delighted to be home with his family and spent most of his time with them. He reacquainted himself with the children he had left behind and spent the summer visiting with old friends and relatives. The war was still on, however, and it was a difficult time for most Americans. Inflation and taxes made it hard to make a living, and everyday necessities were in short supply.

Soon after Adams arrived home, the town of Braintree sent him to Cambridge, Massachusetts, as a delegate to the state constitutional convention. There was no national constitution yet, but each state had to choose its own form of government. The convention eventually chose Adams to draft the constitution. The Constitution for the Commonwealth of Massachusetts set out the system of checks and balances that Adams felt was so important to a stable government. The constitution provided for a bicameral legislature, which is a lawmaking body divided into two parts, a senate and a house of representatives. These two legislative chambers would each balance the power of the other.

Also, he called for a separation of legislative, executive, and judicial powers. What Adams produced stands today as the oldest functioning written constitution in the world.

As happy as he was to be back home in Braintree, Adams did not hesitate when Congress reappointed him to France in October 1779. This time he was chosen as minister plenipotentiary to negotiate peace and commerce treaties with Britain. To go to Europe as a peacemaker was a great honor for Adams. He was treated with more respect by Congress this time, with a salary of 2,500 pounds and his own official secretary, Francis Dana. Another secretary, John Thaxter, joined them. Adams once again brought John Quincy, who was now twelve years old, as well as his son Charles, who was nine years old.

Once again the Adamses faced dangerous adventures at sea. Two days after setting sail, their ship, the *Sensible*, sprang a leak. In the second week, the ship hit a violent storm, which left it leaking so badly that two

After Francis Dana (1743–1811) worked as Adams's secretary, he served as minister to Russia through the end of the Revolution. He was elected to Congress in 1784 and was appointed chief justice of Massachusetts in 1792.

The Alhambra from the Albay, an 1835 lithograph by James Duffield Harding, shows Spain's mountainous countryside. Adams and his party trekked over similar terrain in the winter of 1779–1780 as they made their way across the Pyrenees from El Ferrol, Spain, to Paris, France.

pumps were needed, with everyone on board working to keep the water out. Since another storm or an encounter with enemy ships would leave them no chance of survival, they had to head to the nearest friendly port, which was in Spain.

On December 8, 1779, the *Sensible* docked in El Ferrol, in northwestern Spain. Having no patience to wait for the ship to be repaired, John Adams decided to travel the rest of the way to Paris by land. He was warned against the dangers of this journey, which involved a difficult wintertime trek over the Pyrenees, but he was determined to set off immediately. One week after landing in El Ferrol, John Adams and his two boys, along with Francis Dana, John Thaxter, and some Spanish guides, set off into the mountains on rickety carts drawn by scrawny mules. On the way, most of the travelers came down with severe colds. "We go along barking and sneezing and coughing as if we were fitter for a hospital than for travelers on the road," Adams wrote in his diary. In a letter to Abigail, Adams admitted that he had made a mistake when he decided to come by land.

Adams was shocked by the living conditions of the Spanish peasants he saw along the way. He noticed families living in houses together with mules, hogs, and birds, and people dressed in rags: "Nothing appeared rich but the churches, nobody fat but the clergy." The travelers were warmly welcomed everywhere along the route. Spain had just entered the war on the side of France and the American colonies, and its people cheered the representatives as they passed through the towns.

They finally reached Paris on February 9, 1780, nearly two months after leaving El Ferrol. Adams immediately enrolled his sons in boarding school. Then he went with Thaxter, Dana, and Benjamin Franklin to meet with the Comte de Vergennes. Adams's job was to work out the terms of a peace with Britain as soon as the war ended, and Franklin was still negotiating assistance from France in the war effort. Adams was pleased with Vergennes's reception this time, and reported to Congress that the comte was "so decided . . . in the Course of this Conversation in their declarations to pursue the War with vigor, and afford effectual Aid to the United States." In truth, Vergennes distrusted Adams and believed that he would make peace with Britain behind France's back. Furthermore, he resented Adams's assertiveness and determined to put the American minister in his place. By mid-February, Adams realized that Vergennes's plan was to keep the United States pitted against Britain for France's own advantage.

Unsettled by the American minister's confidence, Vergennes put limits on Adams's job that made him virtually useless. He insisted that Adams keep his peace mission a secret from the British, and that Adams do nothing until he received orders from the French ambassador to America. Adams bristled at instructions from Vergennes. He did not want France to control the terms of the peace between America and Britain, nor did he want America to be dependent on another country. With nothing else to do, Adams dedicated himself to writing articles for French and British newspapers, explaining the American cause. He wrote to Congress almost daily, reporting on European politics and naval activities. He also wrote frequent letters to Abigail in Massachusetts and to his sons in boarding school.

This lithograph shows the library in the Château de Versailles, which housed France's Ministry of Foreign Affairs. The Comte de Vergennes had offices there where he would have written the letters he exchanged with Adams.

In June 1780, Vergennes engaged Adams in an exchange of letters regarding problems with American currency. Three months earlier, Congress had reduced the value of the dollar in hopes of improving America's struggling economy. Vergennes objected to the measure and requested that Adams ask Congress to make an exception for French merchants. Adams replied that such an exception would unfairly favor foreign merchants over Americans. Insulted by Adams's contrary stance, Vergennes refused to deal with Adams anymore

 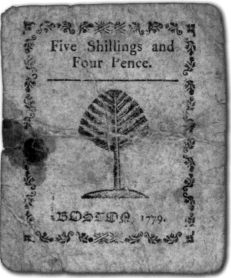

Congress did not have power over states' domestic affairs, such as printing money. This caused problems with trade, as each state printed its own currency. Shown here is a Massachusetts five-shillings-and-four-pence bill from 1779. The front (*left*) depicts a rising sun. The back (*right*) shows a pine tree.

and sent the offending letters to Franklin. Franklin sent the letters to Congress, along with a letter in which he explained Vergennes's reaction and criticized Adams's conduct.

Sensing the lack of support from both Vergennes and Franklin, Adams left Paris for the Netherlands. He hoped to gain Dutch aid for America, in hopes of lessening America's dependence on France. Adams and his sons arrived in Amsterdam in late July 1780. By September, Congress had officially assigned Adams as interim representative to the Netherlands. Five months later, they made him minister plenipotentiary to negotiate a treaty.

During the next two and a half years, Adams tirelessly petitioned the Dutch for recognition of America's independence. His stubborn temperament and his energy were better suited to this more direct mission than to his work in Paris. He made friends in financial circles and tried to obtain loans for the American war effort. He also made friends in the Dutch press and wrote articles to convince the Netherlands to take America's side. Britain had declared war on the Netherlands, but the Dutch were anxious for peace and were reluctant to take America's side in a larger war against Britain. Nothing came of all the talk of financial help, and the Dutch government refused to receive Adams as the representative of an independent nation. Finally, on May 4, 1781, he presented a sixteen-page appeal for help directly to the president of the Dutch States General. Adams did this independently, and he broke the rules of diplomacy. He risked his whole mission on the States General's answer.

In the summer of 1781, Congress appointed Adams's secretary, Francis Dana, minister to Russia. His job was to persuade the Russian government to recognize America's independence. The Russian court conducted diplomatic business in French, but Dana spoke little of the language. John Quincy, at fourteen years old, had mastered French, so Dana took him to St. Petersburg to serve as his secretary and translator.

Adams reluctantly sent Charles away from Amsterdam as well, as the young boy's health was poor and he missed his mother.

During this time, the French ambassador to America, Chevalier Anne-Cesar de la Luzerne, had persuaded Congress that Adams's conduct was harming America's chances for peace. De la Luzerne bribed at least one member of Congress to have Adams removed from his commission as sole negotiator for the peace treaty. Instead of removing him entirely, Congress added four other agents to the mission, Benjamin Franklin, John Jay, Thomas Jefferson, and Henry Laurens. Congress also agreed that the treaty for peace between America and Britain would have to meet with France's approval.

Adams learned of these decisions in late August 1781. Perhaps as a result of this blow, combined with the fatigue of his hard work, he became very sick and nearly died. He recovered some of his health by October but was still depressed by the failure of his mission and Congress's treatment of him. He was also lonely without his sons. He longed to return to Abigail and to his farm in Braintree.

6. Victory and Peace

In Yorktown, Virginia, on October 19, 1781, a combined army of American and French forces under George Washington won a decisive victory over Britain. The British general Cornwallis and more than seven thousand British troops surrendered. The French naval assistance that John Adams had stubbornly lobbied for proved vital to the victory.

The news reached the Netherlands on November 23. Adams's perseverance with the Dutch finally paid off as a result of this victory. Realizing that the Americans would now win the war, the Dutch finally accepted Adams as the official representative of an independent nation on April 19, 1782. Four days later, at a party in Adams's honor, the Spanish ambassador to the Netherlands said that by gaining official recognition of the United States' independence, Adams had "struck the greatest blow that has been struck in the American cause, and the most decisive. It is you who have filled this nation with enthusiasm. It is you who have turned all on their heads." In May, Adams established the world's first U.S. embassy in Amsterdam. The United States now had its own official

Around 1836, Louis Charles Auguste Couder painted this depiction of the surrender at Yorktown. Cornwallis *(second from left)* is shown surrendering to Washington *(center)*. This American victory ended the fighting and secured the success of the Revolutionary cause.

headquarters for diplomacy. This was one of the proudest moments in Adams's diplomatic career.

In October 1782, Adams joined John Jay and Benjamin Franklin in Paris to settle the peace terms with Britain. This was a happier time, as Adams liked Jay and was getting along better with Franklin. The ministers were less dependent on France's support, and the three ministers agreed to defy Congress's instructions and conduct negotiations without Vergennes's authority. The American diplomats met with British diplomats to settle the boundaries of the new nation. In September 1783, they signed the Treaty of Paris, which stated "His Britannic Majesty acknowledges the said United States . . . to be free, sovereign, and independent states."

By the war's end, Adams had not seen his wife or daughter for three years. He still had work to do in Europe, but now that the war with Britain

This portrait of John Jay (1745–1829) was painted by Gilbert Stuart around 1783. Jay was a key negotiator for the terms of the Treaty of Paris.

was over, the seas were safer to cross. He was determined that they live again as a family. On June 20, 1784, Abigail and Nabby Adams set sail for Europe, leaving the two youngest children, Charles and Thomas Boylston, with Abigail's sister Elizabeth. It was a rough voyage, but they arrived safely on the British coast. Then they made their way to London for a happy reunion with John and John Quincy, who had returned

Following spread: This anonymous unfinished painting entitled *Signing of the Treaty of Paris* was created around 1820, after the 1784 original by Benjamin West. From left to right are John Jay, John Adams, Benjamin Franklin, Henry Laurens, and William Temple Franklin.

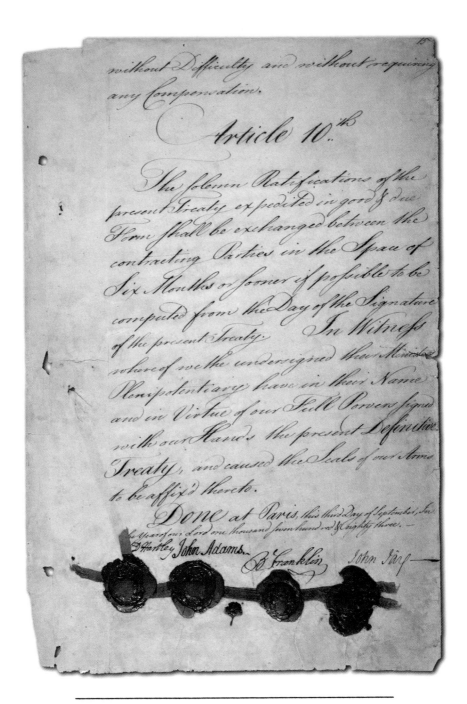

John Adams signed the Treaty of Paris. The treaty states that Britain recognizes the independence of the United States. It set the terms for peace between Britain and the countries that had fought with the United States, including France, Spain, and the Netherlands.

from Russia. The next day the family set off for their new house in Autcuil, a village just outside of Paris.

With the war over and his family beside him, John was happier than he had ever been. Around the same time, Thomas Jefferson came to Paris to work on commercial negotiations with Adams and Franklin. Adams enjoyed working with Jefferson, and the two became close friends. Abigail and the children adored Jefferson as well, and he visited the family often.

Thomas Jefferson had a very different lifestyle than the Adams family had. The commissioners' salary of 200 guineas, which is about $15,000 in present-day currency, was hard to live on, but the Adamses were used to living modestly. Jefferson came from a wealthy background and had always lived elegantly. He spent much of his time shopping, buying new French clothes for himself, his daughter, and his servant, as well as buying silver forks, wine, and scientific models. Over the course of his two years in France, he bought two thousand books. Gradually Jefferson fell deeply into debt.

There were other significant differences between the two revolutionaries. Adams was outspoken and stubborn, but Jefferson hated to argue. Adams was short and overweight; Jefferson was tall and thin. Both men professed a hatred of slavery, but Jefferson owned more than two hundred slaves. Adams believed that the ideal result of independence should be a strong and balanced central government. Jefferson felt that states' rights

France did not impress Abigail Adams at first. Used to managing a whole farm alone, Abigail was frustrated by the number of servants that French society expected her to employ. She believed that the French were too devoted to appearances, and she wrote to her sister that in French society "to be out of fashion is more criminal than to be seen in a state of nature [naked], to which the Parisians are not averse."

Abigail's opinions about France changed as time passed. She became enchanted with French theater and opera and grew to view French life as similar to those types of performance. Although she preferred simple, modest clothes for herself, Abigail also admired the beautiful craftsmanship of French clothing.

and individual liberties were the most important thing to fight for. Despite these dramatic differences, a deep friendship existed between the two throughout their time together in Europe.

Ever since the peace had been settled, rumors had circulated of electing Adams as the first U.S. minister to Britain's government seat, the Court of St. James. There was a dispute in Congress over this appointment, as some argued that Adams was not right for the job because of his ego and temper. Adams had always struggled to control his vanity, and he was deeply hurt when he learned of the debate, but he finally received the appointment in April 1785. At the end of May, John, Abigail, and Nabby set off for London. John Quincy went home to Massachusetts to attend Harvard. The family was sorry to leave France, where they had been so happy. They were especially sad to part with Thomas Jefferson, to whom they had all grown so close.

This anonymous portrait of King George III (1738–1820) was painted in 1831.

Shortly after his arrival in London, John Adams was given private audience with King George III. Adams felt deeply moved as he stood before the man who had been a symbol of tyranny during the Revolution. He was meeting with the British as the representative of the independent United States. His voice quivered with emotion as he began his speech, "The appointment of a minister from the United States to Your Majesty's Court will form an epoch in the history of England and of America." In a letter to John Jay, Adams recorded the King's reply: "I will be very frank with you, I was the last to consent to separation; but the separation having been made, and having become inevitable, I have always said, as I say now, that I would be the first to meet the friendship of the United States as an independent power."

Although they were pleased to live once again in a country where people spoke English, the Adamses found that life in London was hard. Adams's new salary was even smaller than his salary had been in Paris, and the family struggled to maintain a dignified lifestyle. They found their treatment by the English cold and patronizing, and Adams was shunned by British statesmen. Many British believed that the new nation would fail and that American independence could not last. The press ridiculed Adams for this, referring to him as a nobody and an impostor.

Adams spent three years in London trying to work out trade agreements and the withdrawal of British troops from American land. The American economy was in trouble, and British shipping restrictions against the United States made things worse. Largely ignored by the British ministry, Adams made little progress. He was also embarrassed by the fact that the United States still owed money to the British from prewar debts. He spent a lot of time trying to obtain Dutch loans to pay these off.

Jefferson was facing similar troubles in Paris. The United States lacked the power and respect needed to make demands, and the two diplomats were frustrated. They began writing letters to each other discussing the problems they both faced and tried to find solutions together. One problem they both struggled with was the menace to shipping on the Mediterranean caused by the Barbary pirates of North Africa. In July 1785, pirates from Algiers seized two American ships and forced the twenty-one American sailors on board into slave labor. It was an accepted practice in most of Europe to pay huge amounts of cash to the pirates to prevent such attacks. John Jay told Jefferson and Adams to negotiate with the Barbary States, but they had no money on hand for the necessary bribes.

Jefferson came to London in March 1786 to meet with Adams and a diplomat from Tripoli, part of modern-day Libya, to negotiate protection from the pirates. The mission was a failure because they couldn't raise money for the bribe. The Barbary pirates would remain

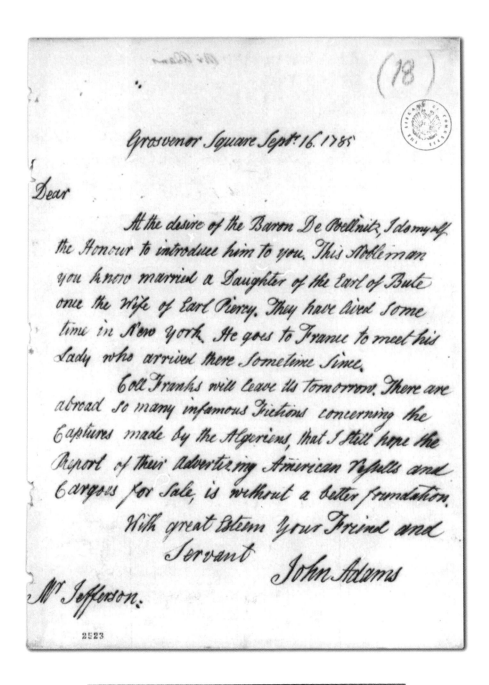

In this letter from Adams to Jefferson, dated September 16, 1785, Adams shares with Jefferson the struggles of his diplomatic post. Adams describes his frustration concerning the Barbary pirates.

a problem for the United States into the nineteenth century. Although Jefferson's visit to London proved fruitless, Adams and his family were delighted to see Jefferson again. Abigail threw several dinners in Jefferson's honor, and Adams joined him on a five-day tour of English gardens in the countryside.

One day Adams went to see his old friend Jonathan Sewall, who had left America during the Revolution. They greeted each other as dear old friends, though Sewall still hated the Revolutionary cause. Most loyalists who had moved to Britain during the war had had a hard time in their adopted country. Although loyalists were hated in America for their loyalty, British society never accepted them, either. Sewall had become a bitter hermit. The reunion saddened Adams, and he believed that the Revolution had ruined Sewall's life.

7. Back Home to America

On March 30, 1788, John and Abigail Adams left London to return home to Massachusetts. The Adamses purchased and moved into a larger house not far from their old farm. Much had changed in America during the ten years John Adams had been abroad. America's population was growing steadily. People were at work building new bridges and ships. The United States had a constitution and was about to elect its first president. Adams absorbed himself in farmwork on his land, but rumors were already circulating about his next public office.

In February 1789, George Washington was unanimously elected as the first president of the United States. Under the rules at the time, the runner-up in an election would become vice president. John Adams was nominated for president and was the runner-up, and so he became vice president. On April 13, the fifty-three-year-old statesman left for the capital in New York, in a grand procession accompanied by cannon salutes and more than forty carriages. On the journey through Massachusetts and Connecticut, crowds lined the roads to cheer their new vice president. He took office in New York City's grand Federal Hall on April 21, 1789.

Adams presided over Washington's inauguration on April 30. Crowds filled the streets as Washington rode to Federal Hall in a majestic yellow carriage pulled by six white horses. After taking the presidential oath of office in the Senate chamber, President Washington gave his inaugural address. Many of the wit-

Amos Doolittle created this copper engraving of Washington's inauguration in 1790. Washington can be seen taking his oath on the balcony of Federal Hall in New York City. New York City was the capital of the United States from 1789 to 1790, when it was moved to Philadelphia. Washington, D.C., became the capital in 1800.

nesses were moved to tears to see this revered general lead the young country into the next phase of its development.

One of the main roles of the vice president was to act as president of the Senate. Adams's job was to moderate debates in the Senate, but he could not vote unless there was a tie. He was not supposed to join in debate, and this restraint proved very hard for such an opinionated, outspoken man. One of the first questions that arose was how the nation should address its president. Like many in the Senate, Adams believed that the president needed a title of dignity and honor to symbolize his authority. He believed that Washington should be called "His Majesty the President." Someone else suggested "His Highness the President of the United States and Protector of the Rights of the Same." Other senators, and most Americans, felt that something more plain was appropriate, to emphasize the contrast between the United States and the monarchy it had rebelled against. The debate went on for nearly one month, and Adams made a bad impression on the Senate. Instead of merely moderating, Adams took one of the most active roles in the debate and lectured the Senate on his views. In the end, Adams lost the debate and the Senate voted for the simple title "The President of the United States."

Adams was widely mocked for his determined stance, and one senator suggested that Adams be given the title of "His Rotundity," making fun of Adams's plump figure. His critics called him a monarchist and accused him of being tainted from his time in the royal courts of Europe. This charge would plague Adams for the rest of his career. Adams's misstep ended up further limiting his role in the president's cabinet. Washington was advised to keep his distance from Adams, because the vice president had made himself so unpopular.

Adams eventually settled into his passive role, and he served Washington loyally through the president's two terms in office. Adams did a good job keeping order in the Senate and never missed a session. By the end of his vice presidency, Adams had cast thirty-one deciding votes in the Senate, more than any other vice president has since that time.

Life became easier in June 1789, when Abigail joined him in New York. The two were also happy to be near their daughter Nabby, who was now married and living in New York with her husband and children. The second Adams son, Charles, had graduated from Harvard and was studying law in New York. In August 1790, the U.S. capital moved to Philadelphia, and Adams set up a house there. Abigail joined him in the fall.

George Washington was adored by the American people when he took office, but political factions started to form during his first term as president. One of the main challenges for the young country was to unite interests on a national scale rather than on a state or a regional level. Many felt that the federal government was a dangerous threat to individual liberties. Two factions broke out around this issue. The Federalists believed that a strong central government was the only way to hold the country together. The Republicans believed that the rights of states were most important and saw a strong central government as a form of monarchy. Thomas Jefferson and James Madison would emerge as the leaders of the Republican Party, which bears little relation to today's Republican Party. Alexander Hamilton,

This 1793 Federalist cartoon, entitled *A Peep Into the Anti-Federal Club* shows Jefferson (*standing center right*) making a speech. In the speech, the anti-Federalist Jefferson is depicted as power hungry and asserting states' rights at the expense of the welfare of the United States.

the treasury secretary, would lead the Federalists. Eventually the points of view came to be referred to as Jeffersonian and Hamiltonian.

These party divisions worried Adams, and he was determined to take no part in them. He was loyal to the president, and therefore aligned with the Federalists, but he disagreed with many Federalist policies. Among those policies were maintaining close ties to Britain and keeping standing armies. Because George Washington was so well loved, nobody dared to criticize him directly. Instead much of the anti-Federalist criticism was aimed at

Adams. Even his old friend and former collaborator Thomas Jefferson criticized him for being part of the Federalist Party and denounced him as a monarchist. Their friendship cooled as a result.

Washington suffered more criticism during his second term in office. Some Republicans denounced him as a monarchical figure. France was now at war with Britain, and Washington issued the Proclamation of Neutrality. This angered the Republicans, who supported France. They felt that the president was allying himself with Britain and betraying the ideals of the Revolution. Britain created more trouble by attacking neutral ships that were bringing supplies to the French West Indies.

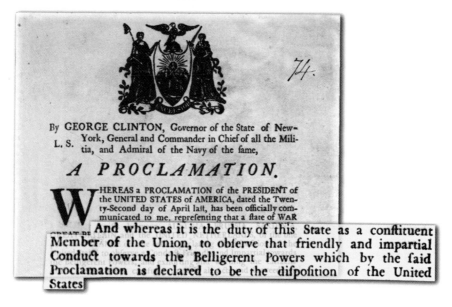

The Proclamation of Neutrality declared that the United States would not get involved in the war between France and Britain. Drafted by New York governor George Clinton, it declared the United States' intention to "observe that friendly and impartial conduct towards the belligerent powers."

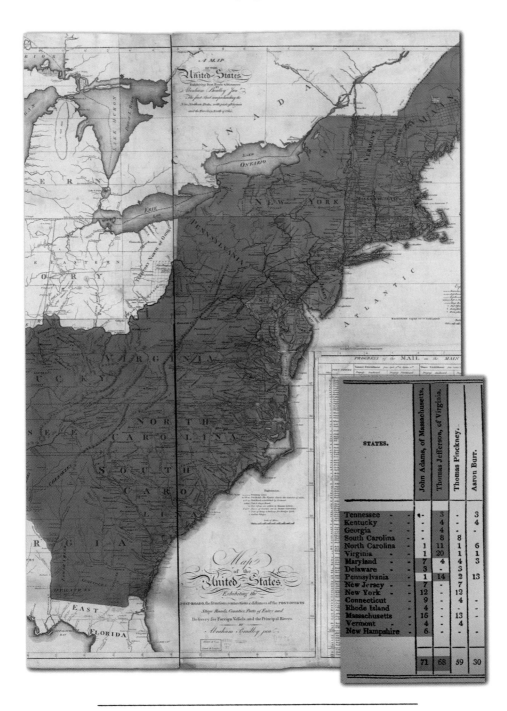

STATES.	John Adams, of Massachusetts.	Thomas Jefferson, of Virginia.	Thomas Pinckney.	Aaron Burr.
Tennessee		3		3
Kentucky		4		4
Georgia		4		
South Carolina		8	8	
North Carolina	1	11	1	6
Virginia	1	20	1	1
Maryland	7	4	4	3
Delaware	3		3	
Pennsylvania	1	14	2	13
New Jersey	7		7	
New York	12		12	
Connecticut	9		4	
Rhode Island	4		4	
Massachusetts	16		13	
Vermont	4		4	
New Hampshire	6			
	71	68	59	30

This map shows the distribution of votes in the tight 1796 presidential race between Adams (*red*) and Jefferson (*blue*). Some states distributed their votes to more than one candidate. *Inset*: This chart shows how each state voted for all of the candidates.

Those who supported France wanted to go to war with Britain. Instead Washington sent John Jay to London to negotiate and avoided the war.

After eight years as president, Washington was tired of public office and of the troubles that came with it. Adams was next in line to run for the presidential nomination for the Federalist Party, and Jefferson ran against him as a Republican. It was the practice at this time for candidates to take no part in their campaigns. Adams retired to his farm to wait out the storm. Jefferson did the same in Monticello, his estate in Virginia. Even with both candidates out of the picture, this presidential race was ugly. Republicans called Adams an aristocrat and a royalist. Federalists called Jefferson a traitor. Hamilton turned against Adams as well, secretly urging electors to vote for Adams's running mate, Thomas Pinckney, instead of Adams. Adams won the election by a narrow margin of three votes, and Jefferson came in second. This meant that Adams's political opponent was now his vice president.

8. The Presidency

John Adams was inaugurated as the second president of the United States on March 4, 1797, in Philadelphia's House Chamber of Congress Hall. In contrast to Washington's grand inaugural entrance, the new president arrived in a simple carriage, drawn by only two horses. He wore a plain gray broadcloth suit without fancy buttons or knee buckles.

In his inaugural speech, Adams declared his hope to reconcile "various political opinions . . . and virtuous men of all parties and denominations." He hoped to form a new partnership with his old friend and vice president, Jefferson. Sadly the party quarreling only got worse. The factions were so wrapped up in their divisions that their party loyalties were stronger than their loyalty to the president. Adams had maintained Washington's cabinet out of loyalty to the first president's administration, but the men in the cabinet took their orders from Alexander Hamilton, who had resigned as treasury secretary in 1795. Adams's own vice president, Thomas Jefferson, was more interested in winning a victory for the Republicans than in collaborating with the president.

Amos Doolittle created this engraving of President John Adams in 1799. The border displays the seal of each state, along with its population and number of senators and representatives.

Realizing that he had no reliable support within his government, Adams depended instead on Abigail's advice.

Tensions with France continued to grow, and these problems, which became known as the Quasi-War, dominated Adams's presidency. The United States attempted to maintain its neutrality, but the French were angry that Americans would not assist them in the war with Britain, and France attacked American ships in the Caribbean. Although a war with France was looking likely, Adams wanted to try for reconciliation. A few days after taking office, he told Jefferson of his plans to send two ministers to Paris to join Charles Cotesworth Pinckney. Pinckney was a Federalist, and Adams wanted to create a bipartisan, or two-party, commission to promote cooperation within the government. He had already chosen Elbridge Gerry, who was not affiliated with either party, and he wanted Jefferson's friend James

This anonymous portrait of Charles Cotesworth Pinckney (1746–1825) was painted around 1795. When asked to provide a bribe for France in the XYZ Affair, he is said to have replied, "No! No! Not a sixpence!"

Madison for the third post. When Adams proposed these appointments to his cabinet, they were outraged. Adams held fast to his position, but Jefferson told him later that day that Madison had refused the appointment. Adams made no further attempts to form a partnership with Jefferson.

On March 13, 1797, Adams found out that the French Directory had refused to see Pinckney and had sent him away from Paris. This was a terrible blow to the peace effort, and Adams realized that he needed to prepare for the possibility of war with France. With his cabinet's support, he began building up the American navy as a defensive measure. This infuriated the Republicans, but Adams assured them that he was still trying to achieve peace. To this end, he sent over the commission he had discussed with Jefferson. In Madison's place he sent John Marshall, a lawyer from Virginia who had served under Washington in the American Revolution.

Adams received no word from the commission for eight months after they left for France. Then in March 1798, the commission sent five dispatches to Philadelphia. It turned out that the French foreign minister Tallyrand had kept the American envoys waiting several days after their arrival in Paris. After finally meeting with them, Tallyrand kept them waiting for an answer. Finally Tallyrand sent three secret agents to ask for a bribe from the envoys. He told them that he would open negotiations with them if they lent the French Republic $10,000,000 and gave him $250,000. The Americans refused.

This incident became known as the XYZ Affair, named for the code names given to the French agents. Tallyrand's treatment of the American ambassadors was extremely disrespectful, and the American public was clamoring for war. Although his Federalist cabinet was eager for war, Adams remained cautious. He continued building up the navy but insisted that it was only for defense. On April 2, Adams received a report that Pinckney and Marshall had left Paris, but that Gerry had stayed behind. The public considered the

The XYZ Affair is illustrated in this June 1798 political cartoon by S. W. Fores. It shows Frenchmen attacking America for money. In the background people representing other European nations look on.

minister a traitor for staying, but Marshall told the president that Tallyrand had threatened that war was certain if Gerry were to leave.

Trying to maintain order in this chaotic and ugly atmosphere, Adams took a step that would mar his presidency. In June 1798, Congress passed the Alien and Sedition Acts, and Adams added his signature to approve it. Under the Alien Act, which was created out of fear of French immigrants, the requirement for U.S. citizenship was now fourteen years' residence where once it had been five. It also gave the president the right to expel any foreigner whom he considered dangerous. The Sedition Act made any "False, scandalous, and malicious" writing against the government, Congress, or the president, or any attempt to "excite against them . . . the hatred of the good people of the United States, to stir up sedition" punishable by fines and imprisonment. Adams and Congress defended the acts as a necessary wartime measure. To the Republicans, and to generations that followed, this was a grave violation of the First Amendment to the Constitution, which guarantees freedom of speech.

Elbridge Gerry finally returned home in October 1798, bearing news that the French wanted peace. On February 18, 1799, Adams declared to the Senate his intention to send Williams Vans Murray to France as minister plenipotentiary. He had consulted no one, not even Abigail, on this decision. The Federalists were furious and opposed any negotiation with France, but made no move to oppose it officially. The following November, after gaining assurance from Tallyrand that the envoys would be treated with respect, Adams sent the new commissioners to France to negotiate the peace. By striking out on his own, both in trusting Gerry and declaring the new commission, Adams had saved his country from an unnecessary war.

To Adams, avoiding the war with France was the proudest achievement of his career. He once wrote to a friend, "I desire no other inscription over my gravestone than, 'Here lies John Adams, who took upon himself the responsibility of peace with France.'"

In the year 1800, Adams's presidential term was coming to a close. The campaign for the next term had already begun in January, and Thomas Jefferson would once again run against Adams as the Republican candidate. As vicious as the last elections had been, this time they were even uglier. While maintaining the appearance of neutrality, Jefferson was secretly spreading campaign propaganda around the country. He hired James Callender to publish a series of horrible attacks against Adams. Since the Sedition Act made it illegal to criticize the president openly, Callender was thrown in jail. Use of the unpopular Sedition Act only made Adams look worse. Although Adams never resorted to the sort of underhandedness and character assassination that characterized Jefferson's campaign, the other

The Alien and Sedition Acts were a series of laws passed by Congress in 1798. There were three Alien Acts. One raised the waiting period for U.S. citizenship, the second allowed for the imprisonment of subjects of enemy nations, and the third permitted the expulsion of any alien the president considered dangerous. Above is the signature page of one of the Alien Acts.

Federalists had no such scruples. They said that Jefferson was a coward and a swindler. They said he was more French than American, that he would lead the country to civil war, and that he was an atheist who mocked the Christian faith.

Federalists turned on Adams, as well, and joined the Republicans in the charges that he was old, addled, royalist, and insane. One of the worst attacks came from Alexander Hamilton, which created a fatal split within the Federalist Party. The election resulted in a tie between Jefferson and the other Republican candidate, Aaron Burr. The decision went to the House of Representatives, and Jefferson eventually won.

In the midst of this political turmoil, Adams also suffered a great personal tragedy. On November 30, 1800, his son Charles died. During their time together in France, Adams had written of his son, "He is a delightful little fellow. I love him too much." Charles became somewhat reckless as a teenager, and was once nearly suspended from Harvard. He might have begun drinking heavily during this period, but eventually he graduated and was successful in his later legal studies. He married Sally Smith, the sister of Nabby's husband, but his drinking worsened, and, by 1799, he had left his wife and two daughters and disappeared. Adams renounced his son at this point, but was later devastated to learn that his son had died of alcoholism at the age of thirty.

The capital was scheduled to move to Washington, D.C., in 1800. The new city on the Potomac River was a bleak scene when Adams went to see it. Still in the midst of construction, the future Capitol's landscape was littered with tree stumps. The sight of slaves laboring on the grounds of the President's House while their masters looked on must have been disturbing to someone who detested slavery. Yet Adams was excited by the buildings coming up, and pleased with the grandness of the President's House.

In his last few months of office, John Adams became the first president to occupy the President's House, which is called the White House today. He wrote in a letter to Abigail, "I pray Heaven to bestow the best of Blessings on this House and all that shall hereafter inhabit it. May none but honest and wise men ever rule under this roof." His words are now carved in the mantelpiece of the White House's State Dining Room.

9. A Long Retirement

At 4:00 A.M. on Jefferson's inauguration day, Adams left the President's House and took a stagecoach home to Massachusetts. It was March 4, 1800, and he was sixty-four years old. As a struggling young lawyer, Adams had once dreamed of achieving greatness. In the forty years that had passed since then, he had helped lead a nation to independence and had convinced powerful governments to recognize that independent nation. He had served as the United States' first vice president and as its second president, meanwhile avoiding a war and maintaining his integrity. Now, having achieved greatness, the old man returned to the ambition that he had held at ten years old. He became a farmer.

Over the years, Adams had expanded the old family homestead to include three houses and 600 acres (243 ha) of land. He took pleasure in working the land. More important, he was now in the constant company of his beloved best friend, Abigail, with no more public duties to tear him away from her.

The house was always filled with family now. Their son Charles's widow and her two daughters lived with them, and Nabby and her four children came to stay one summer. John Quincy returned from Europe with his wife and son and moved close by in Boston.

When he was not farming, Adams spent much of his time reading. A few years into his retirement, he began writing letters again. When Mercy Otis Warren wrote an unflattering portrait of Adams in the first published history of the American Revolution, he wrote a series of long letters to the Boston *Patriot*, trying to defend his character and his role in history. He wrote to his son John Quincy, who traveled the world on diplomatic missions. He also carried on a particularly warm and cherished correspondence with his old friend and fellow Revolutionary Benjamin Rush. Rush encouraged a reconciliation with Thomas Jefferson and in 1812 convinced Adams and Jefferson to write to each other.

"You and I ought not to die, before We have explained ourselves to each other," Adams wrote to Jefferson in 1813. The two former collaborators had not exchanged a word in eleven years, but they soon made up for lost time. Despite the bitterness he felt toward Jefferson for all of his betrayals, Adams felt that the bond of the Revolution would always keep them together. As they remembered through their letters the historical events that they had lived through,

Adams and Jefferson left behind one of the most personal and vivid accounts of the founding of the nation.

Adams lived for a long time, and with the passing of his later years he would see a great deal of tragedy. In 1811, Abigail's sister Mary Cranch died of tuberculosis, and Richard Cranch died of heart failure. Sally Adams became very ill as well. Nabby discovered she had cancer and died two years later, at the age of forty-nine. Thomas Boylston, like his late brother Charles, took to drinking heavily and became an unhappy and unpleasant person. John Adams also mourned the deaths of many of his fellow Revolutionaries, including Benjamin Rush, who died in 1813.

In October 1818, Abigail died of typhoid at the age of seventy-four. The whole town of Quincy went into mourning for her, and an obituary in a Boston newspaper praised her influence on John Adams's career. Adams was devastated by the loss of his wife. Thomas Boylston and his wife Nancy came to live with Adams and to look after the house.

Adams lived to see his oldest son become the sixth president of the United States in 1824. John Quincy had spent nearly his entire life in the public service, first serving as secretary to the minister to Russia at age fifteen. He later served as a minister to Prussia, Russia, and France, as a Massachusetts senator, and as secretary of state under James Monroe. John Quincy had been a source of pride throughout Adams's

Charles Robert Leslie painted this portrait of John Quincy Adams in 1816, just before he became secretary of state. After his presidency, Adams became a congressman.

life. Adams had sensed a capacity for leadership in the ten-year-old boy who had accompanied him on that first voyage across the sea.

As the Fourth of July approached in 1826, Adams, Jefferson, and Charles Carroll were the last surviving signers of the Declaration of Independence. As the "pen" and the "voice" of the Declaration, Jefferson and Adams were invited to speak at countless events commemorating the day. They were now too old and frail to leave their homes, but both were determined to experience one last

Daniel Chester French created this marble bust of John Adams in 1890. Thomas Jefferson kept a similar bust of John Adams on his desk at his home, Monticello.

Independence Day. By July 1, John Adams was dying, and by July 3 he could barely speak. He woke up in the morning on the Fourth, and, when told the date, he said, "It is a great day. It is a good day." John Adams died later that evening. His last words were, "Thomas Jefferson survives." Jefferson had, in fact, died that same afternoon, the fiftieth anniversary of the Declaration of Independence.

•   •   •   •

As one of the leaders of the American Revolution, John Adams made what were probably the two most important appointments for the creation and survival of the United States: George Washington as general and Thomas Jefferson as author of the Declaration of Independence. As the diplomat of a struggling new nation, he strove tirelessly to gain recognition of America's independence. As president of the United States, he averted a war with France that could have brought the new nation to ruin. No major monuments have yet been erected to the second president of the United States. His face is not on any U.S. currency, but John Adams's honesty and independence, his courage and his voice, are still an inspiration more than two centuries after he left office.

Timeline

1735	John Adams is born on October 30 in Braintree, Massachusetts.
1751–1755	Adams attends Harvard College.
1756–1758	Adams studies law in Worcester with James Putnam.
1758	Adams moves to Braintree and begins his law practice.
1761	Deacon John Adams dies.
1764	John Adams and Abigail Smith marry.
1765	Abigail "Nabby" Adams is born.
	John Adams publishes "A Dissertation on Canon and Feudal Law."
1767	John Quincy Adams is born.
1768	The Adams family moves to Boston.
	John Adams defends John Hancock in a smuggling case.
1770	Charles Adams is born.
	John Adams defends British soldiers against charges of murder in the Boston Massacre.
1772	Thomas Boylston Adams is born.
1774	Adams attends the First Continental Congress.
1775	American and British soldiers clash in the Battle of Lexington and Concord on April 19.
	John Adams attends the Second Continental Congress.
1776	Congress approves the Declaration of Independence.

1778	John Adams sails to France as an American minister.
1779	Adams drafts the Constitution for the Commonwealth of Massachusetts.
	Adams and sons John Quincy and Charles sail to Europe.
1780	Adams arrives in Paris to assume duties on an American commission.
	Adams moves to Amsterdam to negotiate a treaty with the Dutch.
1781	American and French forces defeat the British in the Battle of Yorktown.
1782	John Adams opens the world's first U.S. embassy in Amsterdam.
1783	America signs a peace treaty with Britain.
1785	John Adams becomes the first American minister to Britain.
1789	George Washington is elected the first president of the United States of America.
	Adams is elected the first vice president.
	The French Revolution begins.
1796	Adams is elected president of the United States. Thomas Jefferson is elected vice president.
1798	The XYZ Affair occurs in France.
1799	Adams sends a peace commission to France, ending the Quasi-War.
	The French Revolution ends with Napoleon taking power.
1800	Adams becomes the first president to occupy the President's House, later called the White House, in the new U.S. capital of Washington, D.C.

Charles Adams dies.

John Adams loses the presidential election to Thomas Jefferson.

1803   Thomas Jefferson purchases the Louisiana Territory.

1812   America goes to war with Britain.

Adams begins his correspondence with Thomas Jefferson.

1813   Nabby Adams dies.

1818   Abigail Adams dies.

1824   John Quincy Adams is elected president of the United States.

1826   John Adams dies on the fiftieth anniversary of the Declaration of Independence.

Glossary

bicameral (by-KAM-rul) Referring to a law-making body consisting of two parts, such as the Senate and the House of Representatives in the U.S. Congress.

customs (KUS-tumz) A part of the government that collects taxes on goods entering or leaving the country.

defiance (di-FY-unts) Open resistance to authority.

delegates (DEH-lih-gets) Representatives elected to attend a political gathering.

deliberations (dih-lih-buh-RAY-shunz) Long and careful discussions or considerations.

duty (DOO-tee) A payment due and enforced by law or custom, in particular a payment levied on the import, export, manufacture, or sale of goods.

effigy (EH-fuh-jee) A crude figure or dummy that represents a hated person.

epidemic (eh-pih-DEH-mik) The quick spreading of a sickness so that many people have it at the same time.

executive (eg-ZEK-yoo-tiv) Referring to the top branch of government, which includes the president.

French and Indian War (FRENCH AND IN-dee-in WOR) The battles fought between 1754 and 1763 by England, France, and Native Americans for control of North America.

impostor (im-POS-ter) A person who assumes a different character or name to decieve others.

judicial (joo-DIH-shul) Referring to a system of courts of justice.

legislative (LEH-jis-lay-tiv) Referring to the branch of government that makes laws and collects taxes.

legislature (LEH-jis-lay-chur) A body of people that has the power to make or pass laws.

loyalists (LOY-uh-lists) American colonists who were loyal to the British Crown.

neutrality (noo-TRA-leh-tee) Being on neither side of a war.

obituary (oh-BIH-chuh-wer-ee) A death notice often found in the newspaper.

patronizing (PAY-truh-nyz-ing) Behaving as if one is looking down on another.

piety (PY-uh-tee) Strong faith in and strict following of one's religion.

plenipotentiary (pleh-neh-puh-TEN-shuh-ree) A diplomatic agent invested with the full power to conduct business.

reconciliation (reh-kun-sih-lee-AY-shun) Friendship or harmony restored to an unhappy situation.

restrictions (rih-STRIK-shunz) Limits.

sedition (sih-DIH-shun) The act of causing others to turn against the government.

selectman (suh-LEKT-min) A member of the local government board of a New England town.

surveyor (ser-VAY-er) Someone who measures land.

temperance (TEM-puh-rents) Moderation in or abstinence from the use of intoxicating drinks such as alcohol.

Tories (TOR-eez) Loyalists or colonists in support of British rule.

tuberculosis (too-ber-kyuh-LOH-sis) A serious infectious disease that affects the lungs.

typhoid (TY-foyd) An infectious and often deadly disease that is usually caused by unclean food and water.

writs (RITS) Formal written documents.

Additional Resources

If you would like to learn more about John Adams, check out the following books and Web sites:

Books

Adkins, Jan. *John Adams: Young Revolutionary*. New York: Aladdin Library, 2002.

Burgan, Michael. *John Adams: Second U.S. President*. New York: Chelsea House Publishing, 2000.

Herness, Cheryl. *The Revolutionary John Adams*. Washington, D.C.: National Geographic, 2003.

St. George, Judith. *John and Abigail Adams: An American Love Story*. New York: Holiday House, 2001.

Web Sites

Due to the changing nature of Internet links, PowerPlus Books has developed an online list of Web sites related to the subject of this book. This site is updated regularly. Please use this link to access the list:
www.powerkidslinks.com/lalt/johnadams/

Bibliography

Butterfield, L. H.; Marc Friedlaender; and Mary-Jo Kline, eds. *The Book of Abigail and John: Selected Letters of the Adams Family, 1762–1784*. Cambridge: Harvard University Press, 1975.

Butterfield, L. H., ed. *Diary and Autobiography of John Adams. Vol. 1, Diary 1755–1770*. Cambridge: The Belknap Press, 1961.

——, ed. *Diary and Autobiography of John Adams. Vol. 3, Diary 1782–1804, Autobiography Part One to October 1776*. Cambridge: The Belknap Press, 1961.

——, ed. *Diary and Autobiography of John Adams. Vol. 4, Autobiography Parts Two and Three 1777–1780*. Cambridge: The Belknap Press, 1961.

Ellis, Joseph J. *Passionate Sage: The Character and Legacy of John Adams*. New York: W.W. Norton & Company, 1993.

Ferling, John. *John Adams: A Life*. New York: Harry Holt and Company, Inc., 1992.

——. *A Leap In the Dark: The Struggle to Create the American Republic*. New York: Oxford University Press, 2003.

——. *Setting the World Ablaze: Washington, Adams, Jefferson, and the American Revolution*. New York: Oxford University Press, 2000.

McCullough, David. *John Adams*. New York: Simon & Schuster, 2001.

Index

A

Adams, Abigail (wife), 16–17, 41,
51, 53, 57–58, 62, 65, 69, 71,
75–76, 79, 86, 89, 93–94, 96
see also Abigail Smith
Adams, Abigail "Nabby"
(daughter), 17, 65, 71, 79, 92,
95–96
Adams, Charles (son), 17, 55, 62,
65, 79, 92, 96
Adams, Elihu (brother), 6
Adams, John (father), 6, 8, 14
Adams, John Quincy (son), 17, 45,
48, 54–55, 61, 65, 71, 95–97
Adams, Peter (brother), 6
Adams, Sally Smith, 92, 96
Adams, Samuel (second cousin),
20, 24, 26, 33, 36
Adams, Susanna Boylston
(mother), 6
Adams, Thomas Boylston (son), 17,
65, 96
Administration of Justice Act, 32
Alien and Sedition Acts, 89
Amsterdam, the Netherlands, 60,
62–63

B

Barbary States, 73
Boston, Massachusetts, 5, 11,
17–18, 21, 24–26, 28–30, 34
Boston Massacre, 26
Boston Tea Party, 31–32
Braintree, Massachusetts, 5–6, 12,
14, 21, 34, 45, 54–55, 62
Burr, Aaron, 92

C

Callender, James, 90
Cambridge, Massachusetts, 8, 54
Carroll, Charles, 98
Cleverley, Joseph, 7
Coercive Acts, 32
Concord, Massachusetts, 35
Constitution for the
Commonwealth of
Massachusetts, 54
Continental Board of War and
Ordinance, 43
Continental Congress, 33–34
Cornwallis, Charles, 63
Court of Admiralty, 24
Court of St. James, 71
Cranch, Mary, 96
Cranch, Richard, 16, 96

D

Dana, Francis, 55, 57, 61
Declaration of Independence, 40,
98–99
Declaration of Rights and
Grievances, 34
de la Luzerne, Chevalier Anne-
Cesar, 62
Dickinson, John, 37–39
"Dissertation on Canon and Feudal
Law, A," 21

E

El Ferrol, Spain, 56–57

F

Federalists, 79–80, 83, 89, 92
Franklin, Benjamin, 35, 48, 50–51,
53, 57, 60, 62, 64, 69
French and Indian War, 18, 35

G

George III, king of England, 34, 72
Gerry, Elbridge, 86, 88–90
Gridely, Jeremiah, 11, 14, 21, 24

H

Hamilton, Alexander, 79, 83–84, 92
Harvard, 7–9, 11, 21, 71, 79, 92
Hôtel de Valentinois, 49–50
Hutchinson, Thomas, 20, 24, 28, 30

I

Intolerable Acts, 32

J

Jay, John, 62, 64, 72–73, 83
Jefferson, Thomas, 35, 39, 62, 69,
    71, 73, 75, 81, 83–84, 86–87,
    90, 92, 94–96, 98–99

L

Laurens, Henry, 62
Lee, Arthur, 48, 51, 54
Lexington, Massachusetts, 35
Liberty, 25

M

Madison, James, 87
Marsh, Joseph, 8
Marshall, John, 87–89
Martha, 47
Massachusetts Assembly, 32–33,
    41
Massachusetts Government Act,
    32

N

New York City, New York, 21,
    76–77
Noel, Nicholas, 48

O

Oliver, Andrew, 20
Otis, James, Jr., 11, 18, 21, 24

P

Paris, France, 48, 51, 53, 56–57,
    60–61, 64, 69, 73, 86–88

Parliament, 18, 20, 30, 32, 34
Passy, France, 50
Philadelphia, Pennsylvania, 33, 35,
    41, 45, 52, 79, 84, 87
Pinckney, Thomas, 81
Port Act, 32
Proclamation of Neutrality, 83
Putnam, James, 11

Q

Quartering Act, 32
Quincy, Hannah, 14–15

R

Republicans, 79, 81, 83–84, 87, 89,
    92
Rush, Benjamin, 44, 95–96

S

Second Continental Congress,
    35–37, 39–40, 43–45, 52–55,
    58–59, 62, 64, 71
Sensible, 55–56
Seven Years' War, 18
Sewall, Jonathan, 21, 24, 33–34, 75
Smith, Abigail, 16 *see also* Abigail
    Adams
Sons of Liberty, 20, 24, 29–30
Stamp Act, 19–21
Stamp Act Congress, 21
Stockton, Richard, 39

T

Tallyrand, 87–90
Treaty of Paris, 65

W

Washington, George, 35–36, 39, 63,
    76–79, 81, 83–84, 87, 99
Worcester, Massachusetts, 11, 17

X

XYZ Affair, 88

About the Author

Miriam Gross is a freelance writer living in Brooklyn, New York. She was born in Freiburg, Germany, and grew up in Pasadena, California. She studied English at Kenyon College.

About the Consultant

Dr. Edward Fitzgerald is the executive director for the Quincy Historical Society in Quincy, Massachusetts.

Primary Sources

Cover (portrait). *John Adams.* Oil-on-canvas painting, circa 1793, John Trumbull, The White House Collection, courtesy of the White House Historical Association. **Cover (background), page 40.** *Declaration of Independence.* Oil-on-canvas painting, 1817, John Trumbull, Architect of the Capitol. **Page 4.** *John Adams.* Oil-on-canvas painting, circa 1783, John Singleton Copley, © Museum of Fine Arts, Boston, Seth K. Sweetser Fund/Bridgeman Art Library. **Page 7.** *Birthplaces of John Adams and John Quincy Adams.* Watercolor on paper, 1849, G.N. Frankenstein, Courtesy of the Adams National Historic Site, National Park Service. **Page 9.** *A Westerly view of the colledges [sic] in Cambridge, New England.* Reproduction of engraving by Paul Revere, drawn by Josh Chadwick, circa 1900, Library of Congress, Prints and Photograph Division. **Page 13.** Map of Massachusetts. 1775, Printed for R. Sayer & J. Bennett Library of Congress Geography and Map Division. **Page 15.** *John Adams.* Pastel on paper, circa 1766, Benjamin Blyth, Massachusetts Historical Society. **Page 16.** *Abigail Adams.* Pastel on paper, circa 1766, Benjamin Blyth, Massachusetts Historical Society. **Page 19.** *Join, or Die.* Woodcut, May 9, 1754, Benjamin Franklin, Library of Congress, Prints and Photograph Division. **Pages 22–23.** *Views of the area around Boston, New England, 1773.* William Pierie, © HIP/Scala/Art Resource, NY. **Page 25.** *John Hancock (1737–1793).* Oil-on-canvas painting, circa 1816, Finley Breese Morse, after John Singleton Copley, circa 1770, courtesy of Independence National Historical Park. **Page 27.** *The Bloody Massacre Perpetrated in King Street, Boston on March 5, 1770.* Hand-colored engraving, Paul Revere, Library of Congress, Prints and Photograph Division. **Page 29.** John Adams's study. Adams National Historical Site, National Park Service. **Page 33.** *Boston Commissioner of Customs John Malcolm being tarred and feathered by an angry mob.* Engraving, 1794, François Godefroy, Print Collection, Miriam and Ira D. Wallach Division of Art, Prints, and Photographs, New York Public Library Astor, Lenox, and Tilden Foundations. **Page 36.** *A plan of the city and environs of Philadelphia, survey'd by N. Scull and G. Heap.* Engraving, 1777, W. Faden, Library of Congress Geography and Map Division. **Page 37.** *George Washington.* Oil-on-canvas painting, circa 1787, James Peale after Charles Willson Peale, 1779, Courtesy Independence National Historical Park. **Page 42.** Letter from Abigail Adams to John Adams.

March 31, 1776, Massachusetts Historical Society. **Page 46.** *John Quincy Adams.*
Painting, circa 1789, John Ramage, United States Department of State Art
Collection. **Page 49.** *View from the terrace of Monsieur Franklin at Passy of the
first flight under the direction of Monsieur de Montgolfier, 21st November 1783.*
Colored engraving, eighteenth century, French School, Topkapi Palace Museum,
Istanbul, Turkey/Bridgeman Art Library. **Page 52.** *Charles Gravier (1719–87),
the Count of Vergennes.* Pastel on paper, circa 1774, Gustav Lundberg, Château
Blerancourt, Picardy, France/Giraudon/Bridgeman Art Library. **Page 56.** *The Trek
Through Spain, 1779.* Lithograph, 1835, after 1770s engraving by John Frederick
Lewis, James Duffield Harding, Private Collection/Bridgeman Art Library. **Page
59.** Vergennes's library in the Château de Versailles. Chromo lithograph,
nineteenth century, French School, Bibliothèque des Arts Decoratifs, Paris,
France/Archives Charmet/Bridgeman Art Library. **Page 60.** Five-shilling notes.
Paper, 1779, The Robert H. Gore Jr. Mumismatic Collection, Department of
Special Collections, University of Notre Dame Libraries. **Page 65.** *John Jay.* Oil-
on-canvas painting, circa 1783, Gilbert Stuart, United States Department of State
Art Collection. **Pages 66–67.** *The American Commissioners of the Preliminary
Peace Negotiations with Great Britain.* Oil-on-canvas painting, circa 1820, after
Benjamin West's 1784 original, artist unknown, United States Department of
State Art Collection. **Page 68.** *Treaty of Paris* (signature page). 1783, National
Archives and Records Administration. **Page 71.** *King George III.* Painting, 1831,
Anonymous, after William Robinson, The Crown Estate/Bridgeman Art Library.
Page 74. Letter from John Adams to Thomas Jefferson. September 16, 1785,
Library of Congress Manuscript Division. **Page 77.** *Federal Hall.* Copper
engraving, 1790, Amos Doolittle, Library of Congress Prints and Photograph
Division. **Page 80.** *A Peep Into the Anti-Federal Club.* Cartoon, 1793, Art
Resource. **Page 81.** *The Proclamation of Neutrality.* 1793, Library of Congress,
Rare Book and Special Collections Division. **Page 82 (inset).** *Journal of the
Senate of the United States of America.* 1797, Library of Congress, Rare Book and
Special Collections Division. **Page 85.** *President John Adams, framed by the coat
of arms of the United States' sixteen states.* Engraving, 1788–1789, Amos Doolittle,
Library of Congress Prints and Photograph Division. **Page 88.** *Property
Protected—à la Françoise.* Hand-colored engraving, June 1, 1798, published by S.
W. Fores, Library of Congress Prints and Photograph Division. **Page 91.** *The
Alien Act* (signature page). July 6, 1798, National Archives and Records
Administration. **Page 97.** *John Quincy Adams.* Oil-on-canvas painting, 1816,
Charles Robert Leslie, United States Department of State Art Collection. **Page
98.** *John Adams.* Marble, 1890, Daniel Chester French, U.S. Senate Collection.

Credits

Photo Credits

Cover The White House Collection, courtesy of the White House Historical Association; cover (background), p. 40 Architect of the Capitol; p. 4 © Museum of Fine Arts, Boston, Seth K. Sweetser Fund/Bridgeman Art Library; pp. 7, 29 courtesy of the Adams National Historic Site, National Park Service; pp. 9, 19, 27, 55, 77, 85, 88 Library of Congress, Prints and Photograph Division; pp. 13, 36, 82 Library of Congress Geography and Map Division; pp. 15, 16, 42 Massachusetts Historical Society; pp. 22–23 © HIP/Scala/Art Resource, NY; pp. 25, 37 Courtesy Independence National Historical Park; p. 33 Print Collection, Miriam and Ira D. Wallach Division of Art, Prints, and Photographs, New York Public Library Astor, Lenox, and Tilden Foundations; pp. 46, 65, 66–67, 97 United States Department of State Art Collection; p. 47 courtesy of U.S. Navy Art Collection; p. 49 Bibliotheque Nationale, Paris, France/Bridgeman Art Library; pp. 52, 64 Château Blerancourt, Picardy, France/Giraudon/Bridgeman Art Library; p. 56 Private Collection/Bridgeman Art Library; p. 59 Bibliotheque des Arts Decoratifs, Paris, France/Archives Charmet/Bridgeman Art Library; p. 60 The Robert H. Gore, Jr. Numismatic Collection, Department of Special Collections, University of Notre Dame Libraries; pp. 68, 91 National Archives and Records Administration; p. 71 The Crown Estate/Bridgeman Art Library; p. 74 Library of Congress Manuscript Division; p. 80 Art Resource, NY; pp. 81, 82 (inset) Library of Congress, Rare Book and Special Collections Division; p. 86 © National Portrait Gallery, Smithsonian Institution/Art Resource, NY; p. 98 U.S. Senate Collection.

Project Editor
Jennifer Way

Series Design
Laura Murawski

Layout Design
Ginny Chu

Photo Researcher
Jeffrey Wendt